IN GRANITE OR INGRAINED?

What the Old and New Covenants Reveal about the Gospel, the Law, and the Sabbath

Study Guide

for Individuals and Small Groups

Skip MacCarty and Esther R. Knott

Berrien Springs, Michigan

Andrews University Press
Sutherland House
Berrien Springs, MI 49104-1700
Telephone: 269-471-6134
Fax: 269-471-6224
Email: aupo@andrews.edu
Website: http://universitypress.andrews.edu

ISBN 978-1-883925-58-1
Library of Congress Control Number: 2007927684

Printed in the United States of America
11 10 09 08 07 5 4 3 2 1

Project Director Ronald Alan Knott
Project Editor Deborah L. Everhart
Typesetter Thomas Toews
Text and Cover Designer Robert N. Mason

Table of Contents

Introduction v

Chapter 1: The Core Truth of the Covenant(s) 1

Chapter 2: The Universality of the Covenant(s) 5

Chapter 3: How God Defined the New Covenant 9

Chapter 4: New Covenant DNA in the Old Covenant 15

Chapter 5: How the Old and New Covenants Differ 25

Chapter 6: The Two Covenants in History and Experience 37

Chapter 7: Historical and Experiential Applications 45

Chapter 8: Love and Law in the Covenant(s) 55

Chapter 9: Covenant Signs 65

Chapter 10: Covenant Rest 77

Chapter 11: Ten Timeless Truths 85

Chapter 12: Living the Covenants 91

Endnotes 95

Introduction

You are about to embark on an exciting, enriching experience that will equip and empower you as a kingdom builder for God.

In Granite or Ingrained? What the Old and New Covenants Reveal about the Gospel, the Law, and the Sabbath was deliberately written for an audience seeking more than a purely academic study of the old and new covenants. Nevertheless, to adequately cover the subject, the book necessarily contained scholarly material and arguments. So to better enable readers to absorb some of the more scholarly portions of the book, we considered it helpful to prepare this study guide. By working your way through the questions, you will be sure to grasp the concepts. Group discussion will greatly enhance the learning experience and increase the benefits gained from the book.

Because the book contains some weighty study material, it is important to remember that all Scripture, and every theme of Scripture, contains an invitation from God. The prophets and apostles of old were inspired by the Spirit not simply to produce an encyclopedia of religious information. They were to be bearers of a divine invitation to come to Him who is the way, the truth, and the life. God desires that readers of Scripture will recognize His invitation, respond to it, and thereby find true life in Him.

This study guide is organized very simply. Each lesson covers a corresponding chapter of *In Granite or Ingrained? What the Old and New Covenants Reveal about the Gospel, the Law, and the Sabbath,* which will be called the "textbook." The book you are now reading will be referred to as the "study guide." Each lesson begins with a brief summary of the theme of the chapter. The initial questions, designated "For Individual Study," are designed for you to answer on your own as you read the textbook. Most questions are followed by a page number in brackets that corresponds to the page in the textbook where the answer may be found.

The questions at the end of each lesson, designated "For Group Study," are suitable for small-group discussion. It is best if you consider your answers to these questions prior to meeting for group study. Sometimes this section will refer you to questions from the individual study section. These you should prepare for possible discussion with group members. If there are questions you were uncertain about in the individual study section, be sure to discuss these with your group.

Always pray for the presence of the Holy Spirit to help you understand and apply what you are learning. After all, this study of the covenant(s) is not just about information but about transformation. It is the authors' prayer that in every chapter of the book and in every small group discussion of it you will sense God's invitation, respond to it, and accept every blessing God has promised.

For Individual Study:

1. Why have you chosen to read this book on the covenant(s)?

2. What currently comes to your mind when the Bible refers to "law" and "commandments?" [xi]

3. Here is a simple truth: God is love. God loves His entire creation and asks for its full devotion in return.

   Are you willing to spend focused time in study and prayer in order to gain insights and glimpses into God's character and covenant(s)? Write a prayer asking God for specific things you want Him to help you with during the course of this study.

Chapter 1

The Core Truth of the Covenant(s)

We rarely use the word "covenant" in our daily lives. The term may call to mind theological debates with little practical value. How could a discussion of the Bible's old and new covenants possibly contribute anything essential to our understanding of God? Yet, as this chapter points out, we live within covenants every day. We may not use the term "covenant," but we are acquainted with the concept and recognize covenants as vital to quality of life.

God has revealed Himself in Scripture as a God of covenant(s). The more we learn about His covenant(s) with humanity, the better we will understand God Himself. Indeed, the gospel is an expression of God's covenant(s). Simply put, the gospel cannot be fully understood until it is viewed from a basic understanding of His covenant(s).

For Individual Study:

1. Define the Hebrew word "covenant." [1]

   ____

   ____

2. List some of the Old Testament people with whom God made covenants. [1]

   ____

3. What are some covenants/contracts into which we enter? [2]

   ____

   ____

4. How does God's covenant with humanity differ from that of human contracts? [2]

____

a. God promises ____

____

b. God requires ____

____

"The basic idea of the covenant is that of relationship with God,"[1] a relationship characterized by love, trust, and wholehearted commitment. [2]

5. Define "everlasting covenant" as it relates to the Trinity. [3–6]

____

____

____

6. How does this understanding apply to all other covenants? [6]

____

____

7. The term "everlasting" is paired with the word "covenant" sixteen times in Scripture. Explain how the term "everlasting" can apply when the covenants described were made with such people as Abraham, David, and Israel. [7]

____

____

8. Reference to the "everlasting gospel" in Revelation 14:6–7 is specifically addressed to an end-time generation. Where/when was the "everlasting gospel" of Revelation 14:6 first announced to humanity? [8]

____

9. The everlasting gospel constitutes the core truth of the covenant of redemption—God's everlasting covenant.

   This gospel of the everlasting covenant was crafted to "meet humanity in its

   ______________ condition, ______________ us to God, and ______________

   our inheritance in God's eternal kingdom." [9]

   > God's sacrificial commitment during the reign of sin (from the fall of Adam to the second coming of Jesus) to restore humanity to an eternal hope may be termed "the covenant of redemption" or "the everlasting gospel." [10]

10. The gospel preached in the Old Testament era looked forward to the

    coming ______________. [9]

    The gospel preached in the New Testament era, which looked back on the Messiah's atoning

    death and resurrection, was the very ______________ ______________. [9]

For Group Study:

11. Share your answer to Question 1 from the Introduction.

12. From your reading thus far, what do you understand to be the core truth of the covenants? [8–10]

____

____

13. Re-read the story of John Ortberg's daughter on page 5: "Hold you me." Describe a time when you called out similar words to God, when you believed and understood, and then asked for God's self-giving love. [5]

____

____

____

> "Even an infant being held knows, with an understanding deeper than words, that what is being expressed with the body is in fact the decision of the soul: to hold another person in one's heart. *I will seek your good; I will share your joy and hurt; we will know a kind of oneness, you and I.* It is the brief enactment of a covenant. It is a promise of self-giving love." –*John Ortberg*[2]

14. Share something new that you learned from this chapter or some point you have been exposed to before but now see in a new light.

____

____

____

15. As you read this chapter focusing on God's everlasting covenant of love, what affirmed or challenged you in your walk with God?

____

____

____

16. Pray together for the Holy Spirit to reveal God's truths to you and your group as you study, asking that your lives will reflect the love of the everlasting covenant.

Chapter 2

The Universality of the Covenant(s)

Many Christians have been taught that the term "old covenant" in the Bible refers only to God's unique relationship with ancient Israel. It makes them think of a long list of laws that applied to, and were intended for, that nation exclusively. But a fuller understanding of Scripture presents a different picture. God had other nations in mind when He established His covenant with Israel—even nations that seemed to be Israel's enemies.

This chapter presents scriptural evidence showing that God had a dream for the other nations, allowing us to envision the role Israel was called to play in bringing that dream to fulfillment. It may seem like a rather weighty theological study, unless we consider ourselves to be members of spiritual Israel today. Then it becomes immensely relevant.

For Individual Study:

1. God selected certain individuals and made covenants with them and their descendants. How were these select people to view their role in relationship to the covenants? [13]

   a. The privileges of the covenant-bearers included significant blessings and

      heightened ____________________.

   b. The gospel was to be shared, not ____________________.

   c. The covenants were to be inclusive, not ____________________.

2. How is the Divine covenant like a will of God's estate and what are the implications for the executors of the estate? [13]

___

___

   a. Who did God intend to be the beneficiaries of His estate? [13–14]

   ___

   b. Who are the "executors" of His estate? [13–14]

   ___

> "God not only interacts with every individual human being…but also establishes a *public* presence in human history through a covenant people in which he is tangibly manifest to everyone on earth who wants to find him." *–Dallas Willard*[3]

3. As you trace God's mission-directed purpose in the covenants throughout the Old Testament era, how do you see the following covenants as expressions of that purpose? [15–18]

   a. Covenant with Adam (Gen. 3:15) ___

   ___

   b. Covenant with Noah (Gen. 6:18; 9:16) ___

   ___

   c. Covenant with Abraham (Gen. 12:3; 28:14) ___

   ___

> "[Their altars] were a summons to repentant turning from the worship of idols and a call to reconciliation with the God of Abraham, Isaac, and Jacob, the Creator of heaven and earth. They were a missionary-evangelistic witness." *–Meredith Kline*[4]

d. Covenant with Israel at Sinai (Exod. 19:5–6; Ps. 67:1–2; Isa. 26:18)

____

____

4. How was the mission-directed purpose of God's covenant to be made evident in the lives of His followers in the New Testament era? [19]

Matt. 5:13–16 _______________

Matt. 28:19–20 _______________

Acts 17:26–27 _______________

5. Describe in your own words "what might have been" had Israel fulfilled the role God had called them to as His covenant people.

____

____

6. What thoughts does the description of "what might have been" trigger of God's dream/purpose for you?

____

____

7. When you consider the mission-directed covenant that must go to "the nations of the world," who within your circle of influence would God want you to reach with His grace-based, gospel-bearing covenant? List specific names:

_______________ _______________

_______________ _______________

8. Write a prayer asking God to help you be salt and light to the people on your list.

____

____

____

For Group Study:

9. Reflect as a group on your answers to the following questions:
   Question 5
   Question 6
   Question 7

10. Share something new that you learned from this chapter or some point you have been exposed to before but now see in a new light.

____

____

____

11. As you read this chapter focusing on God's intent and dream for other nations, what affirmed or challenged you about God's dream for you?

____

____

____

12. Pray together for those God is calling you to reach. Ask Him to open the doors for you to make some type of contact this week and then report to the group next week.

Chapter 3

How God Defined the New Covenant

When God created us, He encoded us with DNA characteristics that uniquely identify us genetically with a long line of ancestors. Similarly, God encoded His new covenant with identifying marks so that it may be recognized wherever it appears in the Bible. His covenant's DNA is defined in terms of four profound promises, which also constitute the core elements of the gospel. As the new covenant promises are explored in this chapter, ask yourself what it would mean to you if they were all to be fulfilled in your life. Then remember that as you trust God to do so, He can make them a reality!

For Individual Study:

1. Jeremiah, in the Old Testament, prophesied that God would make "a new covenant" with His people. The New Testament took up this theme and for the first time spoke of an "old covenant." Many Bible students, in an attempt to understand the meaning of the "old" and the "new" covenants, have falsely pitted them against each other as follows: [28]

Old Covenant	New Covenant
Old Testament	New Testament
Inferior to the New Testament gospel	The true gospel
Abandoned by God	Replaced the old covenant

2. In preparing to compare and contrast the two covenants, read about the new covenant from both the Old Testament and the New Testament in Jeremiah 31:31–34 and Hebrews 8:8–12.

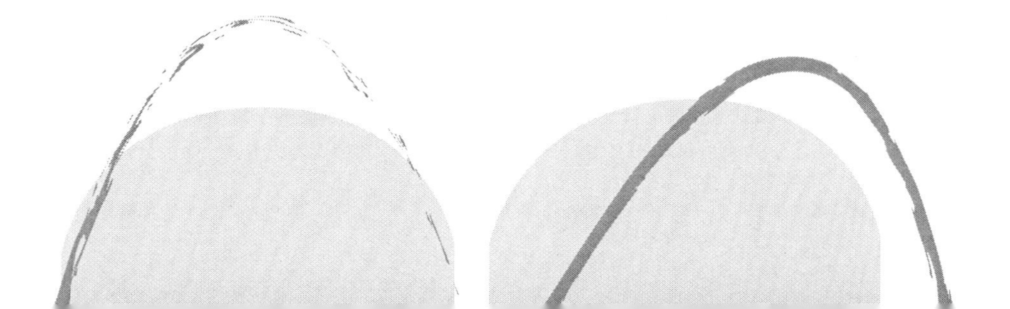

List the four "DNA markers"/Promises/Provisions of the new covenant. [28–32]

Promise/Provision 1: ____________________

____

What theological term describes this? ____________________

Promise/Provision 2: ____________________

____

What theological term describes this? ____________________

Promise/Provision 3: ____________________

____

What theological term describes this? ____________________

Promise/Provision 4: ____________________

____

What theological term describes this? ____________________

3. Why are the DNA markers presented in this particular order? [32–33]

____

____

____

4. Reflecting on Promise/Provision 1: **Sanctification**

   a. What does it mean to have the law "written on your heart"? [29–30]

b. Write about a situation in your life where some law is so internalized that you do not even think of it as a law.

"A time will come in human history when human beings will follow the Ten Commandments and so on as regularly as they now fall to the ground when they step off a roof. They will then be more astonished that someone would lie or steal or covet than they now are when someone will not. The law of God will then be written in their hearts, as the prophets foretold (Jer. 31:33; Heb. 10:16). This is an essential part of the future triumph of Christ and the deliverance of humankind in history and beyond." *–Dallas Willard*[5]

5. Reflecting on Promise/Provision 2: **Reconciliation**

a. What does it mean for you to be "God's man"/"God's woman"?

b. Write about a time in your life when you chose to be reconciled to God.

6. Reflecting on Promise/Provision 3: **Mission**

   a. What insights do the following texts provide about this promise/provision? [30–32]

      Matt. 28:19–20 ______________________________

      ____

      Matt. 24:14 ______________________________

      Rev. 14:6 ______________________________

   b. Why is 2 Corinthians 2:14–15 a key text in interpreting the mission of the new covenant as a description of what the church should be doing until Jesus comes? [31]

      ____

      ____

   c. How does the mission-directed focus of the new covenant establish that the new covenant is always a work in process in anticipation of its complete fulfillment at the second coming of Jesus (cf. Rev. 21:3)? [30–32]

      ____

      ____

> "The correlation of promise and new covenant in Hebrews suggests that the promises of fellowship with God and the universal knowledge of God contained in Jeremiah's oracle are promises, the full realization of which believers can expect only in the world to come." *–Robert Rayburn*[6]

   d. How are you currently seeking to live out the "mission" aspect of the covenant in your life? Or, what do you sense God is calling you to do?

      ____

7. Reflecting on Promise/Provision 4: **Justification**

   a. Trace this provision through Scripture:

      2 Tim. 1:9 ______________________

      Gen. 3:15 ______________________

      Isa. 53:5–10 ______________________

      Matt. 26:28 ______________________

      Heb. 13:21–22 ______________________

   b. "For I will forgive their wickedness and will remember their sins no more." How might your life be different if you truly believed and acted on this promise for yourself? For those around you?

For Group Study:

8. Reflect as a group on your answers to the following questions:

   Question 4 a, b
   Question 5 a, b
   Question 6 d
   Question 7 b

9. Share something new that you learned from this chapter or some point you have been exposed to before but now see in a new light.

10. As you read this chapter focusing on God's promises and provisions, what affirmed or challenged you on your journey?

11. How has God answered your prayers and opened doors for you this past week? Report on any ways in which He has helped you to make contact with people He is calling you to reach.

12. Pray together that we will be faithful partners with God so that the promises/provisions of God's covenant will be a reality in our lives.

Chapter 4

New Covenant DNA in the Old Covenant

Some people look at the Bible and see two gospels—an outmoded one for the Old Testament Hebrews and a different one for Christians today. But as this study shows, the Bible progressively reveals more of the very same message. Every covenant God ever made with humanity presents only one gospel. In our age of theological confusion, nothing illustrates this truth more clearly than a comparison of the law God gave on Sinai with His DNA of the new covenant. While this study is informative, it also brings joy to the heart that is longing for a God who is the same yesterday, today, and forever.

For Individual Study:

1. The covenant God gave His people, Israel, at Sinai is referred to interchangeably by many Bible students as the Mosaic covenant, the Sinaitic covenant, and the old covenant. [34] The use of the term "old" has many definitions (see chapters 6–7), so for clarification we are using the phrase "Sinai covenant" to refer to God's covenant with Israel in the Old Testament.

   Before we look for the "new covenant" DNA promises/provisions in the Sinai covenant, it is important to understand what is included in the Sinai covenant.

   a. What does Moses say God declared as the essence of His covenant? [37]

      Deut. 4:13 ________________________________

b. What reminder did God include in the covenant and what does this reveal about His relationship with Israel? [37]

Exod. 20:2; Deut. 5:6 ____________________

____

c. Exodus 20:22–23:33 elaborates on and gives practical applications of the Decalogue. What name/term does Moses use to refer to these applications? [37]

Exod. 24:7 ____________________

d. What is contained in the book of Leviticus that further clarifies the nature of Israel's covenant relationship with God? [37]

____

____

e. Why is the book of Deuteronomy often referred to by scholars as the "Covenant Book of Israel"? [37]

____

____

Understanding the essence of the Sinai covenant, we can now examine and determine whether it contains the four DNA markers of the new covenant/everlasting gospel.

2. DNA Marker #1—Sanctification (Heb. 8:10): "I will put my law in their minds and write it on their hearts."

   a. In 1 Peter 1:15–16, Peter appealed for Christians to be holy. What relationship does Peter's passage have to the Sinai covenant? (See Lev. 11:45 and 19:22.)

   ____

   ____

b. In the Old Testament, how were people made holy?

Lev. 20:7–8 ______________________________

Exod. 31:12–13 ______________________________

God's call for obedience was premised on His promise to empower people in every way necessary for them to comply. His biddings were His enablings. [39]

c. What sign would remind God's people of how they were to be made holy? [39]

Exod. 31:13 ______________________________

The Sabbath was a symbol and constant reminder to God's people of His promise to sanctify them. [39]

d. Where did God promise He would put His word to enable Israel to obey? [39–40]

Deut. 30:6, 11–14 ______________________________

____

e. Why did David desire to do God's will? [40–41]

Ps. 40:8 ______________________________

f. During the time of the prophet Isaiah, what enabled people to "know what was right"?

Isa. 51:7 ______________________________

God's own promise/provision made it possible for His holy law to be ingrained in the hearts of His people, not just inscribed in granite. [41]

3. DNA Marker #2—Reconciliation (Heb. 8:10): "I will be their God and they will be my people."

a. Leviticus 26 outlines ______________ stipulations God established on Mount Sinai, specifying rewards for ________________ and a series of gradually intensifying

punishments for ________________ disobedience. [41]

b. Leviticus 26 outlines disciplinary interventions. What was God's purpose in designing these? [41]

____

____

"The covenant curses [of Leviticus 26] were, in the initial phase, preliminary judgments from God on his people. They were intended to wake them from their apostate condition, lead them to repentance, and move them toward a positive relationship with God."–*Ranko Stefanovic*[7]

c. Recall a time when someone lovingly disciplined you in order to help you.

____

____

d. What promise did God make to His covenant people in Leviticus 21:12?

____

____

e. God's greatest desire is to be reconciled to His lost children. That is why He is willing to do "whatever it takes" to draw them into covenant relationship with Him. Write a prayer that this reconciling God will do "whatever it takes" so you will be with Him forever.

____

____

____

f. For whom else should you be praying that God will do "whatever it takes"?

____

4. DNA Marker #3—Mission (Heb. 8:11): "No longer will a man teach his neighbor or a man his brother, saying, 'Know the Lord,' because they will all know me, from the least of them to the greatest."

   a. How do the following verses reflect what was to be Israel's role in fulfilling this promise/provision? [42–44]

   Exod. 19:5–6 ______________________________________

   ____

   Gen. 28:14 ______________________________________

   ____

   Ps. 67:1–2 ______________________________________

   ____

   Isa. 49:3, 6 ______________________________________

   ____

   b. Isaiah 49:3, 6 has been called the great commission of the Old Testament. What two New Testament missionaries quoted this commission, showing that they were simply obeying the mission statement of God to His covenant people through the ages? [44]

   Acts 13:46–47 ____________________ ____________________

> "God's election of Israel was therefore an election to a special responsibility to be a blessing to all as a 'kingdom of priests' and a 'holy nation.' This bestowed on Israel the mission to be *priestly mediators* to all Gentile nations, in continuity with the Abrahamic covenant (see Exod. 19:5–6). For this missionary purpose God made a covenant (*berit*) with Israel—a bond of a redemptive fellowship." –*Hans K. LaRondelle*[8]

> "[God's] little kingdom [of Israel] was His bridgehead, never His boundary." – *Derek Kidner*[9]

c. God's covenant people at Sinai were His ambassadors. Through them the world was to hear the passionate appeal of the One who would give His life for their salvation: "Turn to me and be saved, all you ends of the earth" (Isa. 45:22).

   To whom has God called you to be an ambassador for Him?

   ____

   ____

5. DNA Marker #4—Justification (Heb. 8:12): "For I will forgive their wickedness and will remember their sins no more."

   a. What is the circumstance under which the Bible first refers to God as a forgiver of sins or even announces that forgiveness is available? [44]

      Exod. 34:1–7 ______________________________________

      ____

   > It is important to remember that God chose the law as the vehicle in which to reveal Himself as a forgiver. [46]

   b. While characterizing Himself as a forgiver in Exodus 34:7, what kinds of sins did God say He would forgive? [46]

      ____

____

c. According to the following texts, what did God tell Old Testament believers He would do with their sins? [47]

Ps. 32:1–2 ______________________________

Isa. 53:5–6 ______________________________

Isa. 1:18 ______________________________

Mic. 7:19 ______________________________

On the basis of God's revelation and promise in the Sinai covenant, Old Testament believers could experience the reality and assurance that God had forgiven their sins. [46]

d. Who does Paul quote to authenticate and explain his own preaching on justification? [47]

Rom. 4:5–7 ______________________________

6. Sinai covenant as the true gospel of grace

a. Hebrews 4:2 says, "We also have had the gospel preached to us, just as they also did." Who is being referred to here by the pronouns "we" and "they"? [48]

"we" = ________________ "they" = ________________

The gospel embedded in the Sinai covenant was the pure gospel, not "a different gospel." [49]

b. What was Paul's warning about "a different gospel"? [49]

Gal. 1:6–9 ______________________________

____

God's covenant with Israel was fully grace–based, gospel-bearing, and faith-inducing. [49]

7. Having established that the Sinai covenant is grace-based, we must use this understanding to help us interpret John 1:17. Some use this text to convey the message that the covenant God gave at Sinai was based on something other than grace. [50]

   The text in the NIV reads:

   > "For the law was given through Moses; grace and truth came through Jesus Christ."

   The King James and New King James versions insert the conjunction "but" and translate John 1:17 as follows:

   > "For the law was given through Moses, but grace and truth came through Jesus Christ." NKJV

   > "For the law was given by Moses, but grace and truth came by Jesus Christ." KJV

   List some key points from pages 50–53 that you could share with someone who uses John 1:17 to pit "the law given through Moses" against "the truth that came through Jesus Christ."

   ____

   ____

   ____

   ____

   Some points to consider:

   a. Evidence from the Old Testament that the Sinai covenant was grace-based.

   b. Evidence from the New Testament that the Sinai covenant was grace-based.

   c. The problem with the translation that inserts the conjunction "but."

d. Read the context of the passage. (John's use of the word "for" shows that he intended this verse to follow the thoughts in the previous verses.) [50, 52]

e. Notice the point John was trying to make about Jesus: [51]

 The prophets were *bearers* of truth,
 but Jesus was the *source* of truth.
 The prophets testified to God's grace,
 but Jesus, being Himself God,
 was the source of that grace. [51]

f. God's covenants are progressive revelations of His grace. [51]

> "From his fullness we have all received, grace upon grace" (Rom. 1:16, NRSV). [51] Jesus is the ultimate revelation of that very grace expressed in all previous divine covenants. [52]

For Group Study:

8. Reflect as a group on your answers to the following questions:
 Question 3c
 Question 3f
 Question 4c
 Question 7

9. Review Richard Davidson's comments on the terms God used in this passage to identify Himself at the giving of His law. [45–46] Then list two of the terms that especially soften your heart right now, and explain why.

 a. ______________________________

 ____

 b. ______________________________

 ____

10. Share something new that you learned from this chapter or some point you have been exposed to before but now see in a new light.

____

____

____

11. As you read this chapter, which focused on finding the DNA markers of the new covenant embedded in the Sinai covenant, what affirmed or challenged you?

____

____

____

12. Pray together, thanking God for the consistency with which He reveals Himself and asking that we will be faithful in revealing Him to the world.

Chapter 5

How the Old and New Covenants Differ

Even though the old and new covenants have matching DNA characteristics, God Himself did say that the new covenant was not like the one He made with Israel at Sinai (Jer. 31:32). Some Christians use this statement as a basis for throwing out the entire Sinai covenant and starting over completely with the New Testament. Thus it is not surprising to find Christians who study the Old Testament very sparingly, if at all. So, what *did* God mean by saying that the new covenant is not like the one He made with Israel at Sinai?

For Individual Study:

1. In the previous chapters we have seen how the divine covenants are consistent in character: grace-based, gospel-bearing, faith-inducing, and mission-directed. The covenant texts also say that God will make a "new covenant" with His people.

   Read Jeremiah 31:31 and Hebrews 8:8.

   Some interpreters understand "new" covenant to mean a covenant so significantly different in character and purpose from the "old" covenant God made with Israel at Sinai that God intended it to completely overwrite the earlier covenant. But a faithful examination of what is "different" will help us see the consistency of the covenants and experience more fully what God intended.

   From the textbook, list six ways in which the new covenant is "different." [58]

   a. ______________________________

   b. ______________________________

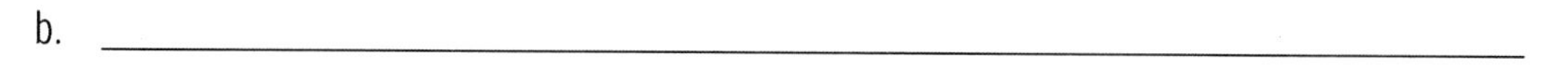

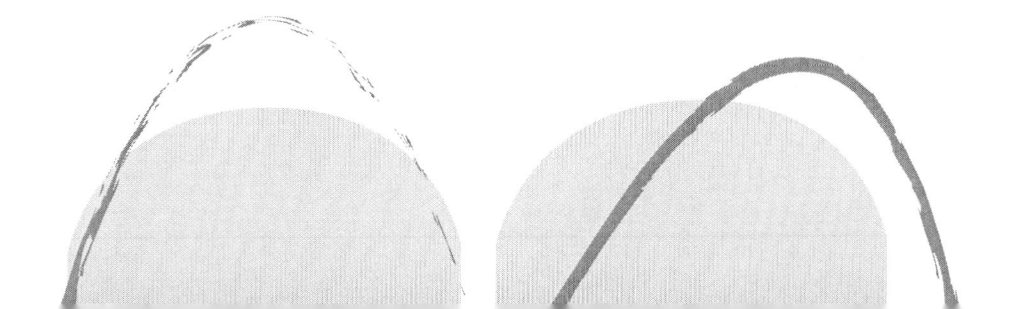

c. ______________________________

d. ______________________________

e. ______________________________

f. ______________________________

2. A Different Response Anticipated [58]

   a. How did those whom God brought out of Egypt respond to His covenant? [59]

      Jer. 31:32 ______________________________

      Heb. 8:9 ______________________________

   b. Read Jesus's parable in Matthew 12:33–37.

      How did the tenants respond to the master's servants?

      ____

      How did the master hope the tenants would respond to his son?

      ____

> Surely, He says, this covenant will be new in the positive way My people respond to it. How could they reject My Son? [59]

3. Like the New Commandment to Love, which Wasn't New

   Sometimes when we use the word "new" to describe something, it does not imply that the old is done away with, but just that there may be a new way of looking at the same (old) thing. Here is an example:

   a. How did the Sinai covenant instruct Israel to relate to God? [59]

      Deut. 6:5 ______________________________

b. How did the Sinai covenant instruct Israel to relate to their neighbor? [59]

Lev. 19:18 ____

c. How did John reiterate these thoughts? Fill in the blanks below. [59–60]

1 John 2:7–8

"Dear friends, I am ______________ writing you a ______________ command but an ______________ one, which you have had since the ______________. This ______________ command is the message you ______________ heard. Yet I am writing you a ______________ command; its truth is seen in him [Jesus]."

2 John 5–6

"I am ______________ writing you a ______________ command but one we have had from the ______________. I ask that we ______________ one another. And this is love: that we walk in obedience to his commands. As you have heard from the ______________, his command is that you walk in ______________."

The Old and New Testaments share the same truths about our relationship to God and humanity. These truths were wondrously illuminated after people saw them lived out in the life of Jesus. [60]

4. A New and More Powerful Revelation

In this section we examine some seemingly contradictory passages. As we discover the continuity we will better understand the "newness" of the new covenant.

a. According to Exodus 6:2–3, what name did God use when He spoke with Moses?

"I am the ________________" [Yahweh].

b. According to Exodus 6:2–3, what name did God use when He appeared to the patriarchs?

"I appeared to Abraham, to Isaac and to Jacob as ________________

________________ [El-Shaddai]."

c. According to Exodus 6:2–3, what name did God not use when He appeared to the patriarchs?

"...but by my name the ________________ [Yahweh] I did not make myself known to

them."

NOTE: Whenever you see the word "Lord" written as "LORD" in your Bible, the term refers to the Hebrew "Yahweh."

d. What name of God is used in connection with the patriarchs in the following passages: Gen. 15:2, 6–7, 18; 21:33; 27:20; 28:13; 32:9?

____

e. So, what was God trying to convey when He told Moses that He had not made Himself known to Abraham "by my name the LORD [Yahweh]"? (Exod. 6:3) List some points you would use in answering this question. [61–62]

____

____

____

____

"The Patriarchs had known *Yahweh* only as the God of promises, but under Moses Israel came to know Yahweh as the *Fulfiller* of His promises. This gave the name *Yahweh* a new character and meaning to Moses that was not known by the patriarchs." –*Gerhard F. Hasel*[10]

5. Making It New and Real to Us

   a. Read Deuteronomy 5:3.

   b. Read the commentaries by Heppenstall, Weinfeld, and Craigie found on pages 62–63. Write some keys points that help us understand this text in light of the theme of the continuity of the covenant(s).

____

____

____

____

The point of Moses's appeal was that Moses's audience might make the covenant given to their fathers their very own, to adopt it and internalize it personally, to assure that it does not remain in granite but rather becomes ingrained within them. [63]

   c. Have you personally embraced God's new covenant promises? When? How?

____

____

If you were raised with Christian parents, when were you able to say, "It was not [just] with my parents that the Lord made this covenant, but with me"?

____

____

d. What can we do to urge our children and grandchildren to seek and to gain a Christian experience for themselves?

______

______

______

______

> God's timeless, universal invitation to salvation takes the form of a new covenant to each new generation. [63]

6. New Ceremonies

a. What ceremony did Abel participate in? [63]

Gen. 4:4 ______

b. How does Exodus 3:18 show us that the Israelites were familiar with the concept of sacrifices and offerings even before Sinai? [63]

______

______

> The Sinai covenant had differed from earlier covenants in the elaborateness of its ceremonial system (introduced in Exodus 25–40 and Leviticus). [63–64]

c. The prophet Daniel prophesied that the coming Messiah would do two things. What were they? [63]

Dan. 9:27 ______

______

d. What new ceremony did Jesus institute to replace the animal sacrifices of the Old Testament? [63]

Luke 22:19–20; 1 Cor. 11:23–26 ____________________

e. What new ceremony replaced circumcision? [63]

Col. 2:11–12 ____________________

Hebrews 7–10 confirms that the animal sacrificial system met its fulfillment in Jesus's once-for-all sacrifice for sin and was no longer to be practiced. [63]

7. Jesus Came in the Middle

a. In the Old Testament times "God spoke to our forefathers through the ____________." [64]

b. In the New Testament times God "has spoken to us by ____________ ____________." [64]

c. What is the most fundamental difference between the Old Testament and the New? [64]

The Old Testament looks ____________ to His coming. The New Testament looks ____________ at it and now anticipates His ____________. [64]

Jesus came in the middle. And it changed everything.

d. Conversion is an experiential form of Jesus's coming in the middle. He comes into the middle of our lives and changes everything. If you have experienced this conversion, write a couple of sentences about how you believe Christ has transformed you.

____

____

____

e. His advent is the epicenter of history. And it expanded the way we look at the Law, the Everlasting Covenant, the Cosmos/Universe, and the Ministry of the Holy Spirit. [64]

1) Floodlight on the Law [65]

a) Ps. 119:142 Your ________________ is truth.

b) John 14:6 Jesus said, "________________ am the way and the truth and the life." (What the law testified to, He was.)

c) Nothing the law said became untrue once Jesus came.

Matt. 5:17–19 "Do not think that I have come to ________________ the Law or the Prophets; I have not come to ________________ them but to ________________ them." (Jesus's life magnified what the law taught.)

2) Everlasting Covenant Personified [66–67]

a) Read Isaiah 42:6–7. Who is Isaiah referring to as the one who will be a covenant for God's people?

____

b) The DNA of the everlasting covenant was Christ's DNA. How are the four DNA markers revealed in the life of Jesus? [67]

Sanctification: ____

Reconciliation: ____

Mission: ____

Justification: ____

3) Cosmically New [67–69]

a) What changed for us because of Jesus's act of righteousness? See Galatians 3:13; Isaiah 53:5–6; Romans 5:17–18; and 1 Corinthians 15:22. [68]

___

___

___

b) Who else was witness to a new revelation of God's love through Jesus's death on the cross? See Colossians 1:20. [68]

___

___

___

In the Christ event God was revealing something breathtakingly new, even to the universe that lies beyond sin's borders, about His everlasting covenant promise and commitment to His creation. [69]

4) The Holy Spirit's New Ministry [69–71]

From the study below we will see how the New Testament writers and Jesus viewed the "newness" of the work of the Holy Spirit in the New Testament period. Even though the Holy Spirit had been operative in the Old Testament, the Holy Spirit's New Testament ministry would make it seem, in comparison, that He had not yet been given in the Old Testament times.

Have you ever given someone a glimpse of something great and then said, "You've seen nothing yet" or "That's nothing compared to what's yet to come"? That is the sense in which the historical old and new covenants describe the work of the Holy Spirit.

a) How was the Holy Spirit operative in the Old Testament?

Gen. 1:1–2 ______________________________

Exod. 31:1–3 ______________________________

1 Sam. 10:6–10 ______________________________

Ps. 51:9–12 ______________________________

Ps. 139:7 ______________________________

Ezek. 36:25–27 ______________________________

Ezek. 37:1–14 ______________________________

b) With the above references in mind, explain what you think John was trying to communicate in John 7:39 and John 16:7.

____

____

____

c) What was the "raw material" available for the Holy Spirit to use in the Old Testament era? [70]

____

____

d) What was the powerful new "raw material" the Holy Spirit had to work with in the New Testament era? [71]

____

> The cataclysmic advent of Jesus, the unifying agent in God's covenant(s) with humanity, made everything that came before it "old" and everything that came with and after it "new." The "old" could never again be fully understood without reading it in the light of the everlasting gospel revealed in Jesus. [72–73]

For Group Study:

8. Reflect as a group on your answers to the following questions:
   Question 4e
   Question 5b
   Question 5c
   Question 5d
   Question 7d

9. Of the six ways this chapter describes how the new covenant differs from the one God made with Israel at Sinai, which one makes the greatest impression on you? How? Why?

   ____

   ____

   ____

10. Is it clear to you that the differences between the two covenants do not involve the four new covenant DNA markers, the core components of the gospel? If not, review the Scriptures and the textbook with your group to help bring clarification and insight.

11. Share something new that you learned from this chapter or some point you have been exposed to before but now see in a new light.

    ____

    ____

    ____

12. As you read this chapter about how the old and new covenants differ, what affirmed or challenged you?

____

____

____

13. Pray that the Holy Spirit will continue to draw you and your group to respond to the One whose coming made/makes all the difference.

Chapter 6

The Two Covenants in History and Experience

No insight about the old and new covenants shared in this book is more important than the one highlighted in this chapter. The Scriptures make a clear distinction between the historical and experiential dimensions of the old and new covenants. Many Christians miss this vital point. Understanding and applying that distinction clarifies the relationship between the covenants.

More than factual accuracy is at stake here. Differing conclusions on this subject can imply different understandings of God, the gospel, and the unity of Scripture. Was God's covenant a divine instrument of salvation, or was it something His people had to be rescued from to find salvation? This chapter seeks to answer that question.

For Individual Study:

1. The old and new covenants have dual applications. What are they? [78]

   a. ______________________________ application

   b. ______________________________ application

2. Define the term "covenant of redemption." [79]

   ____

   ____

   ____

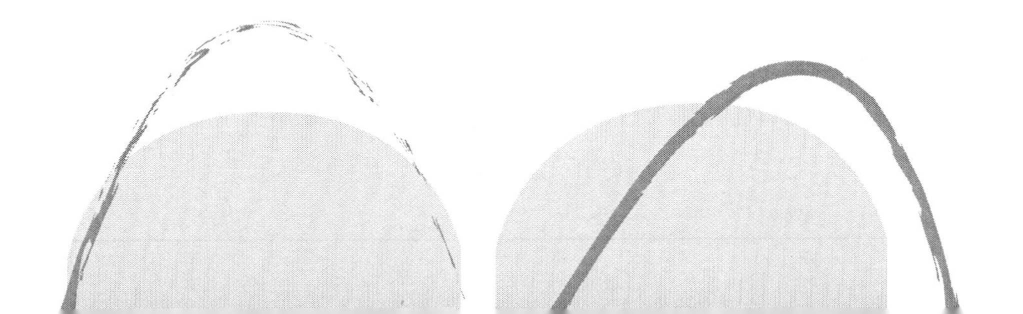

3. The covenant of redemption was divided into two historical periods. What is another term applied to these two historical periods? [79]

   "The two ____________________"

Old Testament historical period	†	New Testament historical period
Historical old covenant		Historical new covenant
Before Christ came		After Christ came

4. Before Christ came there was no Old Testament or old covenant, historically speaking. But after He came, everything prior to His advent was considered "old" and everything that followed was considered "new." [79]

   So, historically speaking, what era, or covenant time frame, are we living in today? [79]

   ____

5. What are some characteristics of the historical **old** covenant? [79–80; see also Table 2 in the textbook, pp. 294–296]

   a. ____

   b. ____

   c. ____

   d. ____

   e. ____

   f. ____

6. What are some characteristics of the historical **new** covenant? [80–81; see also Table 2 in the textbook, pp. 294–296]

   a. ____

b. ____________________

c. ____________________

d. ____________________

e. ____________________

f. ____________________

7. When Paul was discussing old covenant/new covenant concepts, he often was not writing about the two historical divisions of spiritual history (Old Testament and New Testament). To what, then, was he referring? [81]

   Two vastly different ____________ ____________

8. Explain the "experiential **old** covenant experience." [81–82; see also Table 3 in the textbook, pp. 297–300]

   ____

   ____

   ____

   ____

9. Explain the "experiential **new** covenant experience." [82–85; see also Table 3 in the textbook, pp. 297–300]

   ____

   ____

   ____

   ____

10. How is God's law viewed in the experiential new covenant experience? [83]

    Ps. 1:1–3 ______________________________

    Ps. 119:44–47 ______________________________

    Ps. 119:97–104 ______________________________

    Rom. 7:22 ______________________________

    James 2:8–12 ______________________________

11. Briefly review the four promises/provisions of the covenant(s). Describe how Adam, at creation, was a "new covenant" believer. [83–84]

    a. Sanctification ______________________________

    b. Reconciliation ______________________________

    c. Mission ______________________________

    d. Justification ______________________________

> "This grace was given us in Christ Jesus before the beginning of time" (2 Tim. 1:9). Adam's pre-fall experience certainly gives us something to look forward to.

12. What good words did the nation of Israel speak at Sinai? [85]

    Deut. 5:27 ______________________________

13. How did they act on those words a few weeks later? [86]

    Exodus 32; Deuteronomy 9 ______________________________

    ____

    ____

14. More than their words, what did God long for? [86]

    Deut. 5:29 ______________________________

15. Summarize Richard Davidson's comments on this text showing the Israelites' misunderstanding of their ability to stay in covenant relation with God. [86]

    ____

    ____

    ____

16. How can the following words express an experiential **old** covenant experience: "We will do everything the LORD has said; we will obey"? [86]

    ____

    ____

17. How can the following words express an experiential **new** covenant experience while living in the historical old covenant period: "We will do everything the LORD has said; we will obey"? [86–87]

    ____

    ____

18. Explain the following terms: [87]

    a. The old covenant historical era:

       ____

    b. The old covenant experience:

       ____

c. The new covenant historical era:

____

d. The new covenant experience:

____

For Group Study:

19. Reflect as a group on your answers to the following questions:
    Question 8
    Question 9

20. Turn back to Question 10 and have different individuals look up each text and read it aloud.

21. Reflect as a group on your answers to the following questions:
    Question 16
    Question 17
    Question 18

22. What does it mean for you to have a new covenant experience?

____

____

____

23. Share something new that you learned from this chapter or some point you have been exposed to before but now see in a new light.

____

____

____

24. As you read this chapter focusing on the historical old and new covenants and the experiential old and new covenants, what affirmed or challenged you about your own experiential walk with God?

____

____

____

25. Pray together that we will depend wholly on God as the One who alone can bring the inner transformation and conversion of heart and mind that will grant us assurance that He has forgiven us and reconciled us to Himself. Pray that God will also grant us the freedom to obey Him from a heart of love and to share the knowledge of God with others who do not yet know Him as Savior and Lord.

NOTE regarding chapter 7: See the introduction to chapter 7 in this book. Your group members may each wish to select one of the seven scriptural passages listed there and pursue further personal study. When the group meets together again, each member can present what he or she learned about the passage selected.

Notes

Chapter 7

Historical and Experiential Applications

This chapter discusses major New Testament texts that appear to be at odds with the law, including the Ten Commandments, which God gave in the Old Testament era. Applying the historical and experiential distinctions discussed in our last chapter to these texts unveils a remarkable unity in God's plan of salvation. Only when these texts are viewed in terms of experience will we appreciate their true spiritual meaning and sense their divine appeals to the heart.

There is a lot to cover here. Your study group may want to divide the chapter into at least two discussion sessions. This chapter illustrates the scriptural way to interpret many New Testament passages. It may take more than one session to gain a full understanding.

NOTE: Pages 107–128 of the textbook discuss the seven passages below. You may wish to divide the texts among group members and have them evaluate each based on the template of Question 6 in this chapter of the study guide.

1. Not under law but under grace: Rom. 6:14 [107–108]
2. Died to the law: Gal. 2:19 [108–111]
3. Law not based on faith: Gal. 3:12 [111–113]
4. The end of the law: Rom. 10:4 [113–115]
5. The power of sin is the law: 1 Cor. 15:56–57 [115–117]
6. The ministry of death versus the ministry of the Spirit: 2 Cor. 2:14–4:6 [117–126]
7. Law for sinners only: 1 Tim. 1:8–9 [126–128]

For Individual Study:

1. In discussing the old and new covenants, is the emphasis in Hebrews 7–10 primarily historical or experiential? [91]

____

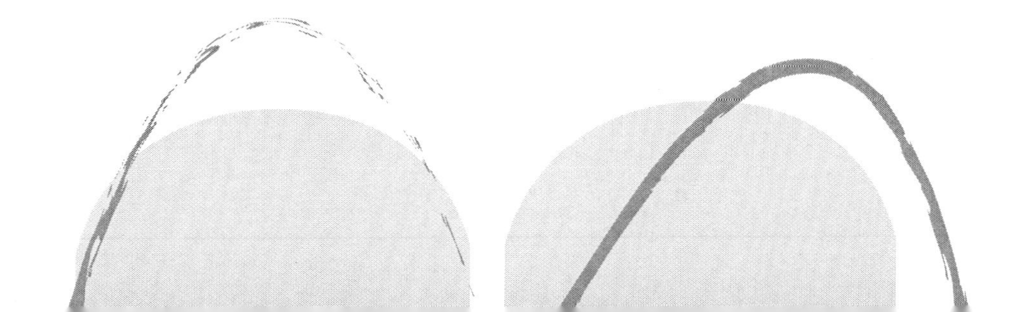

2. In discussing the old and new covenants, is the emphasis in the other New Testament epistles primarily historical or experiential? [92]

____

3. Hebrews 8:13 says: "By calling this covenant 'new,' he has made the first one [referring to the Sinaitic covenant] obsolete."

    a. Occurring in the wider context of Hebrews 7–10, would Hebrews 8:13 most likely be meant to be understood from a historical or experiential perspective? [91–92]

    ____

    b. What elements of the historical old covenant became obsolete once Jesus sacrificed Himself for our sins? [92]

    ____

4. Galatians 4:21–5:1, in which Paul specifically uses the term "two covenants," clearly pits the new covenant against the old covenant. As such, it constitutes a key passage as to what he means by the two covenants and their application to God's law. [93]

    a. If this passage is interpreted from a historical perspective, what does it teach about the covenant God made with His people at Sinai? [93]

    ____

    ____

    ____

    b. Complete the following table to describe the characteristics of these two covenants: [94]

The Flesh	The Spirit
"born in the ordinary way," literally, "according to the ______" (Gal. 4:23, 29)	"Born as a result of a ______," "born by the power of the ______" (Gal. 4:23, 29)
Cannot "share in the ______" (Gal. 4:30)	Receives "the ______" (Gal. 4:30)
"burdened by a yoke of ______" (Gal. 5:1)	______ in Christ (Gal. 5:1)

c. The war between the "flesh" and the "Spirit" is a dominant New Testament theme. From the following texts, describe the contrasts between the two. [95] (We are using the NKJV because it more consistently translates the Greek.)

The Flesh	The Spirit
"That which is born of flesh is ______" (John 3:6)	"That which is born of the ______ is spirit" (John 3:6)
"The righteous requirement of the law might be fulfilled in us who do not walk according to the ______" (Rom. 8:4)	"The righteous requirement of the law might be fulfilled in us who...walk...according to the ______" (Rom. 8:4)
"Those who are in the flesh cannot ______ God" (Rom. 8:8)	"You are not in the flesh but in the ______, if indeed the Spirit of God dwells in you" (Rom. 8:9)
"If you live according to the flesh, you will ______" (Rom. 8:13)	"If by the Spirit you put to death the deeds of the body, you will ______" (Rom. 8:13)
"The ______ of the flesh are...adultery, fornication, uncleanness, lewdness, idolatry,...Those who practice such things will not ______ the kingdom of God" (Gal. 5:19–21)	"The ______ of the Spirit is love, joy, peace, longsuffering,...Those who are Christ's have ______ the flesh with its passions and desires" (Gal. 5:22–24)

d. From the list above contrasting life in the "flesh" with life in the "Spirit," would someone living in the "flesh" be in a saved or lost condition? [95–96]

___

e. Paul describes the old covenant in terms of being "born according to the flesh" (Gal. 4:23, 29) and destined not to "share in the inheritance" with the saints (Gal. 4:30). What then must he mean by the old covenant? [96–99]

___

___

> "The 'covenants' here [Gal. 4:21–31] have *nothing* to do with our division between the Old Testament and the New Testament.... The issues discussed here: legalism versus grace, unbelief versus faith, slavery versus sonship, and the two 'covenants,' have nothing to do with our division between the time before Christ and the time after his coming. These issues are timeless." –*Robert Rayburn*[11]

5. Galatians 3:22–25 refers to a time when "we were held prisoners by the law, locked up until faith should be revealed. So the law was put in charge to lead us to Christ that we might be justified by faith. Now that faith has come, we are no longer under the supervision of the law."

a. Interpreted from a historical perspective, what would this passage say about the law God gave to His people at Sinai? [99–100, 105]

___

___

b. Interpreted from a historical perspective, what would this passage say about "saving faith" (the faith by which a repentant sinner accepts God's justifying grace) before Jesus came in history? [100–101]

___

___

c. In Galatians 3:6, what two texts does Paul quote from proving that "saving faith" was indeed exercised by Old Testament believers? [101]

_______________________ _______________________

d. Describe John Calvin's three uses or functions of the law. [102–103]

First use: Civil _______________________

____

Second use: Tutorial _______________________

____

Third use: Normative _______________________

____

e. How might Calvin's understanding of the second and third uses of the law shed light on Paul's statement in Galatians 3:25 that "now that faith has come, we are no longer under the supervision ['a schoolmaster,' KJV; 'a tutor,' NKJV] of the law"? [103–104]

____

____

____

"Is the law so abolished that we have nothing to do with it? I answer, the law, so far as it is a rule of life, a bridle to keep us in the fear of the LORD, a spur to correct the sluggishness of our flesh, —so far, in short, as it is 'profitable for doctrine, for reproof, for correction, for instruction in righteousness, that believers may be instructed in every good work,' (2 Tim. iii. 16, 17)—is as much in force as ever, and remains untouched." –*John Calvin*[12]

f. According to Richard Davidson, the original Hebrew construction of the Ten Commandments allows for them to be understood either in their traditional portrayal as commands ("emphatic imperative") or as promises ("emphatic promise"). What valuable insight does this grammatical rule suggest as a possible meaning of the statement "now that faith has come, we are no longer under the supervision of the law"? [104]

____

____

g. How do the following texts support the conclusion that God's eternal moral law is as applicable to New Testament believers as it was to Old Testament believers? [106]

Rom. 7:12 ____

Rom. 7:14 ____

Heb. 8:10 ____

h. When Paul uses historical references in his discussions of the covenants, he does so

"primarily to drive home the ____________________ point he makes." [106]

(See the example of this principle in Galatians 3:17 as described on page 106 of the textbook.)

6. Pages 107–128 of the textbook discuss seven additional scripture passages that, if interpreted from a historical perspective, pit the Sinaitic covenant against the new covenant and the law against grace and the Spirit. Choose at least one of those passages and evaluate it based on the following template:

   a. What would be an interpretation of this text viewed from a strictly historical perspective?

   ____

   ____

b. What would such an interpretation imply about God and the unity of both the Scriptures and the plan of salvation?

____

____

c. What would be an interpretation of this text viewed from an experiential perspective?

____

____

d. What would such an interpretation imply about God and the unity of both the Scriptures and the plan of salvation?

____

____

e. What evidence lends support to an experiential rather than a historical interpretation of this passage (e.g., context, other Bible texts, etc.)?

____

____

7. "Believers should never lose sight of the timeless truth that not just the law but salvation and the everlasting covenant itself demand perfection." Why would such a statement not produce neurotic Christians? [128–130]

____

____

____

8. Provide an example of people living in the Old Testament period who possessed a new covenant experience. [130–133]

____

____

____

9. Provide an example of people living in the New Testament period who were in danger of adopting an old covenant experience. [133–135]

____

____

____

> Both the evil "acts of the sinful nature" and reliance "on observing the law" as a means of righteousness and salvation are crucified on the cross of Christ from which grace streams and hope is born. Just as a magnifying glass can focus the rays of the sun to a pinpoint that can start a fire, so the cross of Christ gathers the rays of God's covenant love and focuses them to a pinpoint that can ignite faith and inscribe His law in the heart. [136]

For Group Study:

10. Reflect as a group on your answers to the following questions:

    Questions 4 b, c, d, e
    Questions 5 a, b, c, d, e, f
    Questions 6 a, b, c, d
    Question 7
    Question 8
    Question 9

11. Share something new that you learned from this chapter or some point you have been exposed to before but now see in a new light.

____

____

____

12. As you read this chapter applying the historical and experiential perspectives on the old and new covenants to selected Bible passages, what affirmed or challenged you about your own experiential walk with God?

____

____

____

13. Pray that the Holy Spirit will give you discernment as you seek to appropriately apply the historical and experiential dimensions of the covenants. May the information you learn continue to transform you.

Notes

Chapter 8

Love and Law in the Covenant(s)

Some Christians would have us believe that the Old Testament is primarily a book of law and the New Testament a book of love. Yet the New Testament actually contains more direct commands—or laws—than does the Old Testament. This chapter explores the relationship between love and law as presented in both the Old and New Testaments. It also examines the nature of legalism in contrast to the true freedom to be found in living with Jesus in faith.

> "The law that God had truly given to Israel was, until the coming of the Messiah, the most precious possession of human beings on earth....
>
> "'What great nation is there,' Moses exclaims, 'that has statutes and judgments as righteous as this whole law that I am setting before you today?' (Deut. 4:8). The ancient writers knew well the desperate human problem of knowing how to live, and they recognized the law revealed by Jehovah, Israel's covenant-making God, to be the only real solution to this problem....
>
> "In Ps. 119 and elsewhere we see how the devotee of the law, Jehovah's precious gift, was ravished by its goodness and power, finding it to be the perfect guide into the blessed life in God. It was a constant delight to the mind and the heart.
>
> "We must understand that Jesus, the faithful Son, does not deviate at all from this understanding of the law that is truly God's law. He could easily have written Psalm 119 Himself." *–Dallas Willard*[13]

For Individual Study:

1. Fill in the key words of Robert Rayburn's comments [144]: "It would be a great mistake to view the law as mere regulation; it is ________________ ______________________ and

___________________. The greatest privilege was to be the _______________ _____

__________ and in being his friend there was _______________ _______________.

In the law was revealed the way to _______________ _________ _______________

_______________."[14]

2. What areas of life were covered by the commandments God gave His very large nation at Sinai? [144]

____

____

3. Look up the following New Testament texts which state some particular laws: Matt. 19:16–19; Rom. 13:9–10; Eph. 6:1–3; and James 2:11. To what body of Old Testament law do these New Testament texts refer? [143]

____

4. Deuteronomy was recognized in Israel as the ____________________ Book. [145]

5. Deuteronomy summarizes the _______________ __________________ which is referred to by many as the old covenant. [145]

6. What word occurs in Deuteronomy more often than in any book of the Bible except Psalms, Hosea, John, and 1 John? [145]

____

> Deuteronomy establishes God's love for His people as the foundation for all genuine religious experience. [145]

7. What do we learn about God's love from the Covenant Book of Deuteronomy? [145–146]

   a. Deut. 5:10 ____

b. Deut. 7:8–9 ______________________________

c. Deut. 10:15______________________________

d. Deut. 10:18 ______________________________

e. Deut. 23:5 ______________________________

f. Deut. 33:1–4 ______________________________

8. What is the recurring refrain of Psalm 136?

____

9. Reflecting on Psalm 136, write your own psalm describing how you see God's love reflected in some aspect of God's creation and in how He has led in your personal history. Use a blank page in this manual (e.g., see p. 54) for your composition and be prepared to share your psalm during the small group time. [147]

10. What is the basis for keeping God's commandments? [147]

Deut. 5:10 ______________________________

11. Describe what God was calling Israel to do in each of the following passages of the Covenant Book of Deuteronomy. [148–151]

a. Deut. 6:4–9______________________________

(NT equivalent: Mark 12:32–33)

b. Deut. 7:9 ______________________________

(NT equivalent: John 14:21)

c. Deut. 10:12–22______________________________

(NT equivalent: John 13:34)

d. Deut. 11:1, 13–14, 22–24 ______________________________

(NT equivalent: John 14:21)

e. Deut. 19:8–9 ______________________________

f. Deut. 30:6 ______________________________

(NT equivalent: Phil. 2:13)

g. Deut. 30:19–20 ______________________________

> Clearly any effort to portray the old covenant as weak on love or to portray the New Testament emphasis on love as something unique to the new covenant fails to accurately depict the great emphasis God placed on love in the covenant He made with His people at Sinai. [151] The obedience of the Old Testament believer was inspired by love, motivated by love, rendered in love. Such is the nature of the new covenant experience. [152]

12. Paul indicates that the rule to "Love your neighbor as yourself" includes the sentiments of what other commandments? See Romans 13:9. [151]

a. ______________________________

b. ______________________________

c. ______________________________

d. ______________________________

e. ______________________________

13. Approximately how many commands are in the New Testament? [152]

____

14. Explain the three points that the author draws from his study of the New Testament commands. [152–153]

    a. ____________________

    ____

    b. ____________________

    ____

    c. ____________________

    ____

15. What are some of the direct and specific commands given by Paul? [153]

    Eph. 5:3–5 ____________________

    ____

    ____

16. Many direct and indirect commands are given by Jesus in the Sermon on the Mount. Note the indirect commands given in the following verses: [154]

    a. Matt. 5:22 ____________________

    b. Matt. 6:15 ____________________

> "Remarkably, almost one sixth of the entire Discourse (fifteen of ninety-two verses) is devoted to emphasizing the importance of actually doing what it says." –*Dallas Willard*[15]

17. Read through Table 4 on pages 301–303 in appendix D. Note three of the things listed there that have challenged you or have helped you in knowing how to relate to others.

____

____

____

18. What does James say that reminds us that God intends for us to obey His commands? [155]

James 1:22; 4:17 ______________________________

____

19. What are some of the consequences described in the New Testament for those who unrepentantly continue to disobey God's commandments? [156–157]

a. Matt. 5:19 ______________________________

b. Luke 13:5 ______________________________

c. Rom. 2:9 ______________________________

d. 1 Cor. 6:9 ______________________________

e. 1 Pet. 3:10–12 ______________________________

f. Rev. 6:1–8 ______________________________

"The language of Revelation 6:1–8 parallels 'the covenant curses in the Pentateuch…'" –*Ranko Stefanovic*[16]

The same redemptive curses that were designed to lead Israel to repentance for breaking the Sinai covenant are applicable to the church of the New Testament era. God's plan and way of working with His covenant people is essentially the same in every historical era. [157]

20. What does Rayburn say is the penalty for apostasy in both the Old and New Testaments? [158]

    Expulsion from the ______________________________

21. What was the intent of the covenant warnings and punishments in both the Old and New Testaments? [158–159]

    ____

    ____

22. God's covenants progressively called people to a deeper experience of holiness. In the New Testament God actually raised the moral/spiritual standard. What were some of the reasons for raising the moral bar so high? [159]

    a. Rom. 5:20 ______________________________

    b. Rom. 3:20 ______________________________

    c. Gal. 3:24 ______________________________

23. How might you respond to someone who says, "I don't need any commandments that tell me to 'Do this...Don't do that.' I don't need any other commandment than Jesus." [159–160]

    ____

    ____

24. In Romans 3:21 Paul writes, "But now a righteousness apart from the law, has been made known, to which the Law and the Prophets testify." Explain this text, giving both the historical and the experiential applications. [160–161]

    a. Historical application (Jer. 23:5–6; Heb. 1:1–3; Matt. 5:17–20):

    ____

    ____

b. Experiential application (Phil. 3:9; Rom. 1:5):

____

____

Through a continual and deepening experience, God continued to write His law in the hearts of Old Testament believers that they might delight to do His will in their inward being—which is precisely the new covenant experience. (Ps. 40:8; Isa. 51:7) [161]

25. In Galatians 4:25–5:1 Paul talks about bondage and freedom. What was Paul saying we were in bondage to? And how can we be released from that bondage (Rom. 6:16–18, 20, 22; Ps. 119:44–45; James 2:10–12; 2 Cor. 3:17)? [161–162]

____

____

____

____

Not the commandment itself but one's own experience determines whether the law of God engenders slavery or freedom. [162]

26. What does Peter most likely have in mind when he questioned those who were "putting on the necks of the disciples a yoke neither we nor our fathers have been able to bear"? [162–165]

a. Acts 15:10 ____

____

____

____

b. It is not the number of commandments involved, nor whether they were issued in the Old Testament or the New, that determines whether they engender slavery or freedom. Even one divine commandment can be bondage for "the sinful mind" that is by nature "hostile to God." [164] How so?

Rom. 8:7 ____________________

c. What kind of yoke is the law of God for the heart renewed by the Holy Spirit? [164]

Matt. 11:28–30 ____________________

For Group Study:

27. Reflect as a group on your answers to the following questions:
    Question 7
    Question 8

28. Have the group read Psalm 136 aloud (see Question 9). You might want to divide into two groups. Remember, when God wants to emphasize a point, He uses repetition.

29. Invite those who have written their own psalm for Question 9 to share it with the group.

30. Reflect as a group on your answers to the following questions:
    Question 11
    Question 17
    Question 21
    Question 22
    Question 23
    Question 25

31. Share something new that you learned from this chapter or some point you have been exposed to before but now see in a new light.

____

____

32. Describe the difference between legalism and freedom in Christ.

____

____

33. Why are some religions more prone to legalism than others?

____

____

34. As you read this chapter on love and the law—and legalism in contrast to freedom in Christ—what affirmed or challenged you about the way you view God's law?

____

____

35. Read these excerpts from Psalm 119 together. Ask God to help this be your prayer.

[11] I have hidden your word in my heart that I might not sin against you.
[14] I rejoice in following your statutes as one rejoices in great riches.
[16] I delight in your decrees; I will not neglect your word.
[24] Your statues are my delight; they are my counselors.
[33] Teach me, O Lord, to follow your decrees; then I will keep them to the end.
[34] Give me understanding, and I will keep your law and obey it with all my heart.
[35] Direct me in the path of your commands, for there I find delight.
[45] I will walk about in freedom, for I have sought out your precepts.
[64] The earth is filled with your love, O Lord; teach me your decrees.
[66] Teach me knowledge and good judgment, for I believe in your commands.
[92] If your law had not been my delight, I would have perished in my affliction.
[108] Accept, O Lord, the willing praise of my mouth, and teach me your laws.

Chapter 9

Covenant Signs

The Bible describes several covenants God made with people. He also attached special "signs" to some of these covenants. He ordained the *rainbow* as the sign of His covenant promise to Noah that He would never again destroy the world with a flood. He gave Abraham the sign of *circumcision,* reminding his descendants that God's promises to provide a lineage for His Messiah would not be accomplished by human works, but by His Spirit and through faith. God instituted the *Sabbath* at creation as a covenant sign representing His creatorship of all things and illustrating that personal holiness comes as a result of walking with God. This chapter traces the role of these signs through spiritual history. It especially considers what role God intends for the Sabbath as a covenant sign in the New Testament.

For Individual Study:

1. What are the three covenant signs in this chapter? [171]

   ______________________ ______________________ ______________________

2. In what context does the Bible refer to a rainbow in the following verses? [171]

   a. Gen. 9:8–17 ______________________________

   b. Ezek. 1:28 ______________________________

   c. Rev. 4:3 ______________________________

   d. Rev. 10:1 ______________________________

> It seems reasonable to assume that the rainbow will continue as a symbol of God's faithfulness to His covenant promises throughout eternity. [172]

3. What was God's promise to Abraham? [172]

   Gen. 15:1–5 ________________________________

4. What was the ritual used to confirm the promise? [172]

   Gen. 15:6–18 ________________________________

   ____

5. What was the meaning of walking between the slaughtered animals? [172]

   ____

6. What was unusual about God passing between the pieces? [172]

   ____

7. In his impatience and doubt about God fulfilling His promise, how did Abraham respond? [172]

   Genesis 16 ________________________________

8. In Genesis 17 God took the initiative to renew the covenant. What was the sign of the covenant? [173]

   ____

9. List two things this ritual was to help Abraham and his descendants remember. [173]

   ____

   ____

10. Read Exodus 4:24–26. What do you think God's purpose was in using this drastic action? [173]

____

11. Read Joshua 5:1–9. Of what was circumcision to be a reminder? [173]

____

12. Other nations practiced circumcision. However, it had a different meaning for God's covenant people. Explain that meaning. [173–174]

____

____

> The physical sign in the flesh represented a spiritual transformation of the heart, which God was pledged to accomplish in response to their faith in Him: "The LORD your God will circumcise your hearts and the hearts of your descendants, so that you may love him with all your heart and with all your soul, and live" (Deut. 30:6). [174]

13. What did Moses mean by saying that he had "uncircumcised lips"? [174]

Exod. 6:12, 30 ____

____

14. When David called Goliath an "uncircumcised Philistine," what was he referring to? [174]

1 Sam. 17:26 ____

15. What does Paul say true circumcision is and is not, and how does this relate to an old and new covenant experience? [174–175]

Rom. 2:28–29 ____

____

16. On what basis was Abraham counted as righteous? [175]

    Rom. 4:10–11 ____

17. On what basis would the circumcised and uncircumcised be saved? [176]

    Rom. 4:11–12 ____

18. What was the issue at the Jerusalem council? [176]

    Acts 15:1 ____

19. What decision regarding circumcision was made at the Jerusalem council? [176]

    Acts 15:13–29 ____

> The New Testament clearly states that the physical act of circumcision no longer serves as a covenant sign. [177]

20. The Old Testament rite of circumcision appears to have been replaced by what New Testament ceremony? [176–177]

    Col. 2:11–12 ____

21. In Galatians, Paul refers to circumcision thirteen times, never positively, yet it was not the physical act of circumcision against which he was contending but its ________________ application. [177]

> The bottom line issue in the New Testament is not circumcision or no circumcision but a new covenant experience versus an old covenant experience. [178]

22. The Lord spoke through Moses and gave Israel another covenant sign. What was the sign? [178]

    Exod. 31:12–13, 16–17 ____

23. What two things was the sign to help them remember? [178]

Exod. 31:13 ____________________

Exod. 31:16–17 ____________________

24. When was the Sabbath first given and to whom? [178–179]

Gen. 2:2–3; Exod. 31:17; Mark 2:27–28 ____________________

____

25. Meredith Kline writes [180]: "Observance of the Sabbath by man is thus a confession that

Yahweh is __________ __________ and Lord of all lords. Sabbath-keeping

expresses __________ __________ to the service of his Lord."[17]

26. How did observance of the Sabbath affect life during the week? [182]

Deut. 6:5–7; Ps. 1:2 ____________________

____

27. What evidence do we have that the Sabbath of the fourth commandment was never intended by God to benefit the nation of Israel alone? [182–185]

   a. Gen. 2:2–3 ____________________

      NOTE: The nation of Israel did not exist at creation.

   b. Num. 15:15–16; Isa. 56:3–4, 6–7 ____________________

      ____

      ____

c. Gal. 3:7; Heb. 8:8, 10 ________________________________

____

28. What role were the Old Testament scriptures to fill for New Testament believers? [185–186]

2 Tim. 3:15–17; Acts 17:11 ________________________________

____

29. In two chapters of the New Testament God's covenant is likened to a "will" (Gal. 3:15–18, 21; Gal. 9:15–18, 22, 26). What do these texts suggest about how much of God's covenant(s) in the Old Testament apply to New Testament believers? [186–189]

____

____

____

30. From your reading of pages 189 to 191, explain how it is possible that the natural descendents of Abraham may not be considered Abraham's seed while those not born of Abraham may be considered Abraham's seed (also see Rom. 9:6–7; 2:28–29; John 1:12).

____

____

31. According to Romans 14:1, on what kind of matters was judgment not to be passed? [191]

____

32. What were some of the issues that had come into dispute in the Jewish Christian community at that time? [191] (You will also find endnotes 29–30 on p. 210 very helpful.)

____

The Sabbath instituted at creation and embedded in the Ten Commandments was never a disputable matter. [191]

33. In Colossians Paul refers to "the written code that was against us." What is that "written code" or "bond"? [192]

34. In what way were the things mentioned in Colossians 2:16 a "shadow of things to come"? [192–193]

    Col. 2:17 ________

For more comments from scholars, see appendix C (pp. 285–290).

35. What was the religious background of the Galatians? [194]

    Gal. 4:8 ________

36. What was Paul urging them not to become enslaved by again? [194]

    Gal. 4:9–10 ________

Thomas Aquinas believed that in this passage Paul warns former "heathens" not to return to "the distinction of days, months, years and times which are based on the course of the sun and moon because those who observe such distinctions of times are venerating heavenly bodies and arranging their activities according to the evidence of the stars. [213]

37. Based on the debate at the Jerusalem Council, what were four early church directives to Gentile converts? [197]

________________________ ________________________

________________________ ________________________

> Because the Ten Commandments were taken for granted as universally applicable, the council had no need to specifically instruct Gentile converts not to murder or steal, to be respectfully obedient to parents, or to observe the Sabbath. [198]

38. How would the Gentile Christians continue to be nurtured in their faith? [198–199]

Acts 15:21 ____

____

39. Look up the following passages and note how the book of Revelation alludes to the Ten Commandments. [199–203]

a. Rev. 1:10 (with Isa. 58:13 and Mark 2:28) ________________________

b. Rev. 2:14 ____

c. Rev. 9:20 ____

d. Rev. 9:21 ____

e. Rev. 11:18–19 ____

f. Rev. 12:17; 14:12 ____

g. Rev. 14:7 ____

What passage from the Ten Commandments does Revelation 14:7 allude to?

Exod. 20:8–11 ____

"When the author of Revelation describes God's final appeal to the human race in the context of the end-time deception, he does so in terms of a call to worship the creator in the context of the fourth commandment." –*Jon Paulien*[18]

h. Rev. 15:5 ______________________________

What is the "testimony" referred to in Revelation 15:5? [201]

Exod. 32:15–16; Deut. 10:5 ______________________________

i. Rev. 21:8 ______________________________

40. Revelation 15:3–4 speaks of a time when believers from both old covenant and new covenant eras will join together in singing the (historically old covenant and experientially new covenant) song of Moses and the (historically and experientially new covenant) song of the Lamb. John the Revelator borrows some of his language from Isaiah 66, which describes that same time when people will assemble to worship God throughout eternity. According to Isaiah 66:23, how often does this corporate worship happen? [201–202]

"From one New Moon to another and from one ______________ to another, all mankind will come and bow down before me," says the LORD.

41. Revelation 17–18 speaks of a counterfeit system of religion by using colors that are symbolic.

a. Which colors are used to describe this counterfeit system? [202]

Rev. 18:16 __________ __________ __________ and fine linen.

b. The garb of the high priest in the Old Testament is described with which colors? [202]

Exod. 28:5, 15, 23 __________ __________ __________

__________ and fine linen.

c. What was the predominant color in the high priest's garment? [202]

   Exod. 28:31 ______________________________

d. What color in the high priest's garment is missing from the counterfeit system? [202]

   ____

e. God assigned a very specific meaning to the color blue in the covenant garb of the Old Testament. A blue cord with tassels was to hang from the corners of priestly garments. What was the blue cord with tassels supposed to help the people remember? [202]

   Num. 15:37–40 ______________________________

   ____

   What term does Paul use to refer to the antichrist? [203]

   2 Thess. 2:7–9 ______________________________

> Revelation warns of a counterfeit religious system with a leader who will pose as the world's spiritual high priest, but without a commitment to the commandments of God. [203]

For Group Study:

42. Reflect as a group on your answers to the following questions about the sign of circumcision:
    Question 5
    Question 6
    Question 9
    Question 12
    Question 15

43. Reflect as a group on your answers to the following questions about another covenant sign:
    Question 22
    Question 23
    Question 26
    Question 27

44. Reflect as a group on your answers to the following questions:
    Question 29
    Question 30
    Question 33
    Question 34
    Question 38

45. Of the series of texts in Question 39 noting allusions to the Ten Commandments in the book of Revelation, which one or two most impressed you?

____

46. Share something new that you learned from this chapter or some point you have been exposed to before but now see in a new light.

____

____

____

47. The material on pages 204–206 in the textbook covers responses to several practical concerns regarding the spiritual effect of Sabbath observance. Based on this material and on your own personal experience, share some ways in which keeping the Sabbath of creation and the Ten Commandments could represent either an old covenant or new covenant experience.

____

____

____

> There is spiritual freedom provided in laying aside secular activities at Friday sundown in order to engage worshipful pursuits, with minds directed toward God, family, serving others, and healthful rest until sundown on Saturday as the Sabbath commandment envisions and Jesus's own practice exemplifies. [206]

48. As you read this chapter focusing on God's role for the Sabbath as a covenant sign in the New Testament era, what affirmed or challenged you about your own experiential walk with God?

____

____

____

49. It is possible that as you have studied this chapter the Holy Spirit has been convicting you of some new directions you may need to take in your life. You may be one of God's covenant people who needs to be delivered from workaholism. The Sabbath provides such a rescue when you set it aside as sacred time. Perhaps you have never experienced the rest that Sabbath brings because you observed it in a legalistic way. God calls you to the new covenant experience of the seventh-day Sabbath.

    Share with your group what you believe the Holy Spirit is telling you and pray together that you will each experience a deepening relationship with God as you seek to celebrate God's enduring covenant sign.

Chapter 10

Covenant Rest

God's covenants were designed to draw seekers into a relationship of complete trust in Him. They were never intended merely to convey information about blessings, responsibilities, and consequences. All who respond to His divine invitation—"Come to me…and I will give you rest"—experience a rest of faith. God has offered this covenant rest to everyone since the time of Adam's fall. Those who respond are groomed as a missionary people fit for citizenship in His eternal kingdom. This chapter explores God's invitation to experience His rest and also revisits the sign He gave to represent that rest.

For Individual Study:

1. Complete the following: [217–219]

   a. "My ________________ will go with you, and I will give you ________________."

      (Exod. 33:14)

   b. In repentance and ________________ is your salvation, in quietness and

      ________________ is your strength. (Isa. 30:15)

   c. This is what the LORD says: "Stand at the crossroads and look; ask for the ancient paths, ask where the good way is, and walk in it, and you will find ________________ for your souls." (Jer. 6:16)

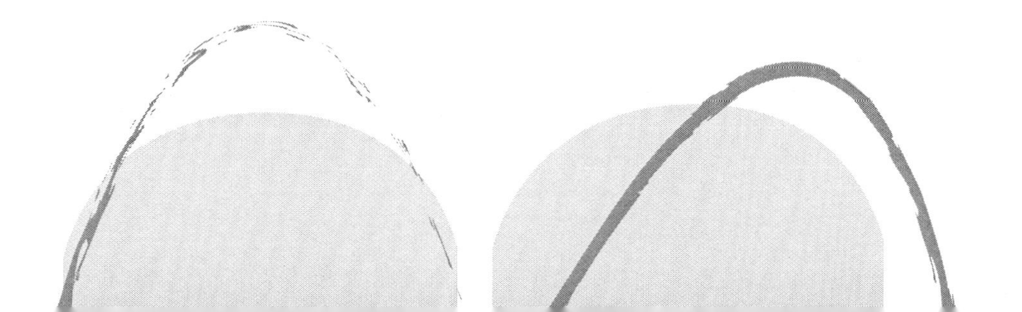

2. What did these patriarchs have in common—Adam, Enoch, Noah, Abraham, and Moses? [218]

   They ________________ in God.

3. Describe what it means to have "rest." [217–218, 226]

   ____

   ____

4. Sabbath is a transliterated word—the sounds of the Hebrew word "Shabaat" and the Greek word "sabbaton" were adopted to make the English word "Sabbath." What is the translation, or meaning, of the word "Sabbath"? [219]

   ____

   Genesis 1:3 might read as follows: "At creation God blessed the seventh day and made it holy, because on it he rested [Sabbathed] from all the work of creating that he had done."

5. The Sabbath commandment is invested with both temporal and spiritual significance. Describe these two. [219]

   a. Temporal significance: ____

      ____

      The rest envisioned in the Sabbath provided physical rest from labor in order to promote deeper spiritual rest in God. [219]

   b. Spiritual significance: ____

      ____

      God intended that in observing the Sabbath, humanity would be drawn by His Spirit more deeply into rest in Him. [220]

6. God had performed mighty acts on behalf of Israel, demonstrating that they could trust Him. How did Israel show that they were not resting/trusting in Him? [220–221]

   a. Num. 14:2–11 ______________________________

   ____

   b. Exod. 17:1–7; Num. 20:1–13 ______________________________

   ____

> It is the nature of God's covenant that no matter how many physical blessings He may shower on us, if we do not trust Him, we will never experience the deep spiritual rest He invites us into in covenant relation with Him. [221]

7. When Israel on the whole failed to enter God's rest, what evidence is there that He did not give up on them? [222]

   a. Ps. 95:7–11 ______________________________

   ____

   b. Ezek. 33:11 ______________________________

   ____

> As Hebrews 11 testifies, countless thousands of Old Testament believers did through the Spirit's enabling put their trust in God, manifest the obedience that comes from faith, and thereby enter and enjoy God's covenant rest. God Himself was their true rest, their true Sabbath. [222–223]

8. What is God's appeal today? [223]

   Matt. 11:28–30 ______________________________

   ____

9. Read Hebrews 3 and 4 before addressing the remaining questions for this lesson.

   Based on Hebrews 3:1–6, who were God's representatives of His grace-based, gospel-bearing, faith-inducing, and mission-directed historical old and new covenants? [225]

   Old covenant ____________________

   New covenant ____________________

10. What warning from the Old Testament community was brought into the New Testament era? [226]

    Heb. 3:7–12 ____________________

11. Why was Israel, as a nation, not able to enter into God's rest? [226]

    Heb. 3:18–19 ____________________

12. Why was the gospel of no value to those to whom it was preached during the time of the Old Testament? [226]

    Heb. 4:1–2 ____________________

13. What specific kind of rest is referred to in Hebrews 4:9? [227]

    ____

14. How did the author of Hebrews link the Sabbath-rest referred to in Hebrews 4:9 with the Sabbath God instituted at creation? [227]

    Heb. 4:4 ____________________

    ____

15. How does Hebrews 4:10 clarify the meaning of this Sabbath-rest?

    ____

    ____

16. Of what is the Sabbath to remind us? [229]

    Exod. 31:13 ______________________________

17. According to Hebrews 4:12–13, how does the word of God make us holy? [230]

    "...it penetrates even to dividing soul and spirit, joints and marrow; it ______________

    the ______________ and ______________ of the heart."

    > Under the supervision of the Spirit, the Word of God in Scripture received by faith searches out and destroys anything in the heart that inclines toward an old covenant experience, and will continue to produce more and still more of the fruit of righteousness that will enable the believer's witness to influence the lives of others toward the kingdom of God and true covenant rest in Him. [230–231]

18. What comfort and promise can we find regarding our great High Priest? [231]

    Heb. 4:14–16 ______________________________

    ____

19. What still remains for the people of God? [232]

    Heb. 4:9 ______________________________

For Group Study:

20. Review with your group the answer to Question 3.

21. The faith experiences of God's covenant people of old were expressions of covenant rest. What aspects of covenant rest do you discover in the lives of the following patriarchs? (See p. 218.)

    a. Adam: ______________________________

    b. Noah: ______________________________

c. Abraham: ______________________________

d. Moses: ______________________________

22. Like the patriarchs, we too sometimes face situations in which we need to rest in God's love and promises, trust and obey when we don't understand, go where we are called, and face ridicule for Christ. Looking at the expressions of "covenant rest" in the previous question, do you see any that you might need in your life right now?

____

____

23. If your story were to be written, what aspect of "covenant rest" might others discover in your life? Share your own experience of "covenant rest."

____

____

24. Reflect as a group on your answers to the following questions:
    Question 5
    Question 6

25. Like the Israelites of old, we sometimes demonstrate a lack of trust in God. How does that prevent us from experiencing the fullness of the covenant rest He offers us?

____

____

26. Share with the group something God has done in your life that has demonstrated to you that you can trust Him.

____

____

27. Reflect as a group on your answers to the following questions:

    Question 7
    Question 12

28. Read Matthew 11:28–30. What steps do you need to take to accept God's appeal in this passage and the passages from Question 7 (Ps. 95:7–11; Ezek. 33:11)?

29. Reflect as a group on your answers to the following questions:

    Question 14
    Question 16

30. Read Hebrews 4:12–13. What evidence have you seen in your life of the double-edged sword of God's word doing its work?

31. Read Hebrews 4:14–16. What is the message in this passage for you?

32. Re-read Shelly Quinn's story on page 229 and respond to it.

33. Share something new that you learned from this chapter or some point you have been exposed to before but now see in a new light.

____

____

____

34. Are you experiencing the rest God offers you in His covenant? Share where you presently discern yourself to be in your spiritual journey with regard to this experience.

____

____

____

> God has so much more for us to experience as we continue to enter into His rest and find our completeness in Him.

35. As you read this chapter focusing on God's invitation to enter into His covenant rest, what affirmed or challenged you about the way you have related to God's Sabbath-rest?

____

____

____

36. Pray together that you will experience the spiritual rest and security that comes to those who trust God. Pray that God will remove any unbelief, disobedience, wrong thoughts, and attitudes that prevent you from entering into His Sabbath-rest and resting from your own works.

Chapter 11

Ten Timeless Truths

This chapter summarizes our conclusions regarding the old and new covenants and presents ten basic truths about the gospel story. These truths apply at some level to all humanity in every era. The promises of God's everlasting covenant have always resided in His heart and will be fully realized at the Second Coming when He restores the physical and relational paradise that Adam lost. As you study this chapter, ask yourself if any of the "ten timeless truths" apply only to people living during one of the covenant eras. You will be able to share your views in the Group Study section.

For Individual Study:

1. Review some of the key points: [235–236]

    a. We can have a new covenant experience whether we live in the historical

    _________________ covenant era, or the historical _________________ covenant era.

    b. When the gospel has been internalized and ingrained, we refer to this as having a

    _________________ covenant experience.

    c. When the gospel is perverted into an external religion, carved in stone, in granite only, this

    is referred to as an _________________ covenant experience.

2. Review the four DNA markers—Promise/Provisions of God's covenant: [236]

   a. Promise/Provision 1 (Sanctification)

      ___

   b. Promise/Provision 2 (Reconciliation)

      ___

   c. Promise/Provision 3 (Mission)

      ___

   d. Promise/Provision 4 (Justification)

      ___

3. Identify each of the "ten timeless truths" and explain how the accompanying scripture references support each truth. [237–241] (We have given a text from the Old and New Testaments/covenants for each truth.)

   a. Timeless truth 1: ___

      ___

      Gen. 1:26–27 ___

      2 Tim. 1:9 ___

   b. Timeless truth 2: ___

      ___

      Isa. 24:5 ___

      Rom. 5:12, 15 ___

Each of us also sins personally and stands guilty before God in judgment. [237]

c. Timeless truth 3: ______________________________

____

Isa. 64:6 ______________________________

Rom. 7:1–6 ______________________________

We must die to the old covenant experience in order to find true life. [238]

d. Timeless truth 4: ______________________________

____

Gen. 3:15 ______________________________

2 Tim. 1:9 ______________________________

e. Timeless truth 5: ______________________________

____

Jer. 31:33–34 ______________________________

Heb. 8:10–12 ______________________________

f. Timeless truth 6: ______________________________

____

Gen. 3:15 ______________________________

Acts 17:24–28 ______________________________

God has planted in every heart a God-shaped vacuum that hungers for a loving relationship with God. [239]

g. Timeless truth 7: ______________________________

____

Isa. 53:1–11 ______________________________

Rom. 3:22–24 ______________________________

h. Timeless truth 8: ______________________________

____

1 Sam. 10:6, 9 ______________________________

John 3:3–6 ______________________________

No person in history has ever been converted apart from the ministry of the Holy Spirit. [240]

i. Timeless truth 9: ______________________________

____

Ezek. 36:27 ______________________________

Rom. 8:4 ______________________________

God's invitation to love Him and keep His commandments was never intended as a call for lost people to do this to be saved, but always as an enabling call to those who are being saved. [241]

j. Timeless truth 10: ______________________________

____

Psalm 67 ______________________________

2 Cor. 2:14 ______________________________

Converted people share Christ's passion for the salvation of lost people. [241]

For Group Study:

4. Share with the group your answers to Question 3. (You may wish to go around the circle and each summarize one of the ten timeless truths.)

5. Do you believe that any of the ten timeless truths would have been applicable to historical New Testament/covenant believers but not so to historical Old Testament/covenant believers?

   If so, which ones? ______________________________

   Explain your answer. ______________________________

   ____

6. Share something new that you learned from this chapter or some point you have been exposed to before but now see in a new light.

   ____

   ____

   ____

7. As you read this chapter summarizing "ten timeless truths," what affirmed or challenged you about God's total commitment to His creation and your relationship with Him?

   ____

   ____

   ____

8. As you have studied and discussed this book on the old and new covenants, what have you discovered that has helped you the most? What questions still remain for you?

   ____

   ____

   ____

9. Pray for each other, thanking God for new understandings and asking that He will make the new covenant experience a reality in your life. Ask God for faith to deal with any unanswered questions, wisdom to find the answers you need, and power to live by the answers you already have.

Chapter 12

Living the Covenants

Our study of God's covenant must come down to one question: What difference does it make in my life? God did not inspire Scripture for the primary purpose of educating our minds, though that is certainly one function of Scripture. He wants it to transform our hearts. It is better to be uneducated and heaven-bound than educated and eternally lost. But God prefers that we be both educated and heaven-bound. That is why we read Scripture and stimulating books and engage in discussions as we have during these past twelve or thirteen weeks. In this last chapter I have shared some ways the Holy Spirit has affirmed me as a child of God while calling me ever higher as an ambassador of His kingdom. Now it is your turn to make the application.

For Individual and Group Study:

> It is one thing to study the covenants, but it is another to let our study impact our lives, leading us to be more Christlike, living to bless others. [246]

1. Looking at the DNA of God's covenant, write how each promise/provision would express itself in your life under an old covenant experience and under a new covenant experience. [246–250]

   a. Promise/Provision 1 (Sanctification): "I will put my law in their minds and write it on their hearts."

      Old Covenant Experience:

      ____

      ____

      ____

New Covenant Experience:

____

____

____

b. Promise/Provision 2 (Reconciliation): "I will be their God and they will be my people."

Old Covenant Experience:

____

____

____

New Covenant Experience:

____

____

____

c. Promise/Provision 3 (Mission): "No longer will a man teach his neighbor or a man his brother, saying, 'Know the Lord,' because they will all know me, from the least of them to the greatest."

Old Covenant Experience:

____

____

____

New Covenant Experience:

___

___

___

d. Promise/Provision 4 (Justification): "For I will forgive their wickedness and will remember their sins no more."

Old Covenant Experience:

___

___

___

New Covenant Experience:

___

___

___

2. What did you learn from this chapter that helped you gain a new perspective on the purpose of living out the new covenant experience?

___

___

___

___

3. As you have been engaged in this study, in what specific ways have you discovered the Holy Spirit speaking to you regarding your own personal relationship to God?

____

____

____

4. Pray together the following benediction:

   May the God of peace,
   who through the blood of the eternal covenant
   brought back from the dead our Lord Jesus,
   that great Shepherd of the sheep,
   equip you with everything good for doing for his will,
   and may he work in us what is pleasing to him,
   through Jesus Christ,
   to whom be glory for ever and ever.
   Amen.
   Hebrews 13:20–21

Endnotes

1. Robert Rayburn, "The Contrast Between the Old and New Covenants in the New Testament" (PhD thesis, University of Aberdeen, 1978), 227.

2. John Ortberg, *Everybody's Normal Till You Get to Know Them* (Grand Rapids, MI: Zondervan, 2003), 36.

3. Dallas Willard, *The Divine Conspiracy: Rediscovering Our Hidden Life in God* (San Francisco: Harper Collins, 1998), 333.

4. Meredith G. Kline, *Kingdom Prologue: Genesis Foundations for a Covenantal Worldview* (Overland Park, KS: Two Age Press, 2000), 378.

5. Willard, 142.

6. Rayburn, 196.

7. Ranko Stefanovic, *Revelation of Jesus Christ: Commentary on the Book of Revelation* (Berrien Springs, MI: Andrews University Press, 2002), 216.

8. Hans K. LaRondelle, *Our Creator Redeemer: An Introduction to Biblical Covenant Theology* (Berrien Springs, MI: Andrews University Press, 2005), 34.

9. Derek Kidner, *Psalms 73–150* (London: Inter-Varsity Press, 1975), 275.

10. Gerhard F. Hasel, *Biblical Interpretation Today* (Washington, DC: Biblical Research Institute, 1985), 22.

11. Rayburn, 127.

12. John Calvin, *Calvin's Commentaries: Romans–Galatians* (Wilmington, DE: Associated Publishers and Authors, n.d.), 1898.

13. Willard, 141.

14. Rayburn, 47.

15. Willard, 137.

16. Stefanovic, 215; cf. Jon Paulien, "The Seven Seals," in *Symposium on Revelation—Book 1*, 223ff. (*Daniel and Revelation Committee Series 6* [Silver Spring, MD: Biblical Research Institute, 1992]).

17. Kline, 39.

18. Jon Paulien, "Revisiting the Sabbath in the Book of Revelation," *Journal of the Adventist Theological Society* 9, nos. 1 & 2 (1998): 185.

If you have suggestions for increasing the usefulness and relevance of this study guide, please send them to maccarty@andrews.edu for consideration and possible inclusion in future editions of the book.

Notes